Phonics Reader

Intermediate

Harcourt School Publishers

www.harcourtschool.com

Printed in the United States of America

ISBN 10 0-15-368093-8

ISBN 13 978-0-15-368093-9

    4 5 6 7 8 9 10 0983 16 15 14 13 12 11 10 09

CONTENTS

2

3

A Walk in the Woods

by Barbara Diaz
illustrated by David McPhail

Kim and Tip loved fall. They loved to
go for walks in the woods.

Kim loved walking in the fall leaves.
Tip loved sniffing the fall leaves.

Kim loved the apple trees south of the woods. She picked some apples.

Tip loved chipmunks. He loved looking for chipmunks.

"Look over there, Tip!" said Kim.

"I see a chipmunk! Can you find his tree?"

"Look at the chipmunk zip up that big
tree!" said Kim. "We will sit for a bit."

Kim and Tip did not make a noise.

Then Kim said, "When will you come
down, chipmunk?" They could see the
chipmunk, but it did not come down.

"We have to go, Tip," said Kim.

"We have to walk back. I loved picking apples. You loved sniffing leaves. And you and I loved seeing a chipmunk!"

My Week at Camp Wonder

by Deborah Eaton
illustrated by Howard Weliver

Mom,
    I like everyone at summer camp a lot.
Look what I got! It likes to get in my suitcase.
It is <u>not</u> poisonous. Doc Ross said so when it
bit Counselor Bob.

                Todd

Mom,

My sock can hop! Look at this! It could win medals for hopping. What makes it hop? Something is in the sock. It is a frog! A friend got the frog in there. Now there is a big spot on it. Will you get the spots out?

Todd

11

Mom,

   I did something to my suitcase. It had all my rocks in it. Now it has a rip in it. Do not get mad! I can fix it. See?

                              Todd

Mom,

I lost my harmonica in the pond. I practiced as I sat on a big rock. Then Counselor Bob said, "STOP!" And DROP! I lost it. Everyone cheered. They like my songs a lot.

Todd, the Summer
Camp Kid

Mom,

I have something in my cabin. It's a dog! He got on my cot. Then everyone ran. It was odd! He looks like a hotdog. He's my friend. Mom, may I have him? He can sit in my suitcase. Ask Pop!

Todd

Todd,

    You have to come back now. This box is for the hotdog dog. Get him in it for the trip back. We miss you, summer camp kid!

Mom

The Promise

by Susan McCloskey

illustrated by Laura Freeman

Crump's Toy Shop was packed.

Lun was there with his mom.

"Mr. Crump, will this plane's engine start?"
asked Lun.

"No, but this plane's will," said Mr. Crump.
"Here are the directions."

So Lun and his mom bought that one.

Bud was in the toy shop with his dad.

"Mr. Crump, will this crane's engine start?" asked Bud.

"No, but this crane's engine will," said Mr. Crump. "Here are the directions."

So Bud and his dad bought that one.

Mr. Crump's cat, Muffin, was sitting
in the sun.

She was tugging one of the toys.

What was that buzz? What was that hum?

Muffin twitched. She looked up. It was a
bug! She liked bugs.

Muffin jumped up. What fun!

"That cat can run!" said Bud.

"Yes," said his dad, "but that bug can fly."

"That cat can jump," said Lun.

"Yes," said his mom, "but that bug can fly."

Mr. Crump said, "The bug can fly. Muffin can't, but do not worry. She'll get that bug. That's a promise!"

The bug landed on a plane. So did Muffin.
Smash! The plane was flat.

The bug landed on a shelf. So did Muffin.
Crash! The toys spilled all over.

Muffin looked for the bug. Was it in the
rug? She dug and dug.

At last Muffin grabbed the bug.
She dropped it into Mr. Crump's hand.
Mr. Crump hugged Muffin. Then he
let the bug go.
So long, bug!

Lun helped Mr. Crump pick up the toys.

"Muffin has a lot of fun hunting for bugs!"
Lun said.

Mr. Crump grinned. "Yes. Muffin likes to
hunt. She will not stop until she gets her bug.
That's a promise!"

Muffin sat in the sun. What was that buzz?
What was that hum? It was a bug!

What fun! Muffin liked bugs.

Gram's Plant Parade

by Susan McCloskey
illustrated by Melanie Hall

My name is Blake, and this is my gram. Gram adores plants.

Gram plants in any vacant vase. She plants in hats and caps. She plants in cake pans and brass vats. She plants in frames and crates.

Look! One plant is sprouting in a skate with no mate!

"Blake!" says my gram. "Look at the
station on the corner. Do you see what I see?"
"No, Gram. What do you see?" I ask.
"Vacant land to plant!" says Gram.

Gram takes a sack. I take the spade. We go to the station on the corner.

Gram has bulbs in the sack. She takes bulbs from her pockets, too.

"Now hand me my spade, Blake," she says, "and stand back. I have to plant!"

As Gram plants, we attract stares. Recognizing that I am anxious, Gram pats me on the back.

"Blake, aren't you glad we're sprucing up the station?" she says. "I can't stand a drab, bare landscape!"

"Gram, you amaze me! When will the bulbs be sprouting?" I ask.

"In the future," Gram says. "Then we'll see a plant parade!"

At last the future comes to pass!

Gram and I go to gaze at her plant parade. Now it's the plants that attract stares! One man thanks Gram for sprucing up the corner.

"Will you retire from planting now, Gram?" I ask.
"Retire? Not me!" Gram gazes around the square.
"Look!" she says. "I see vacant land!"
Now I want to share Gram's plant craze.
I know a new plant parade is in our future!

The NOT-So-Boring Night

by Kathryn Corbett

illustrated by Wong Herbert Yee

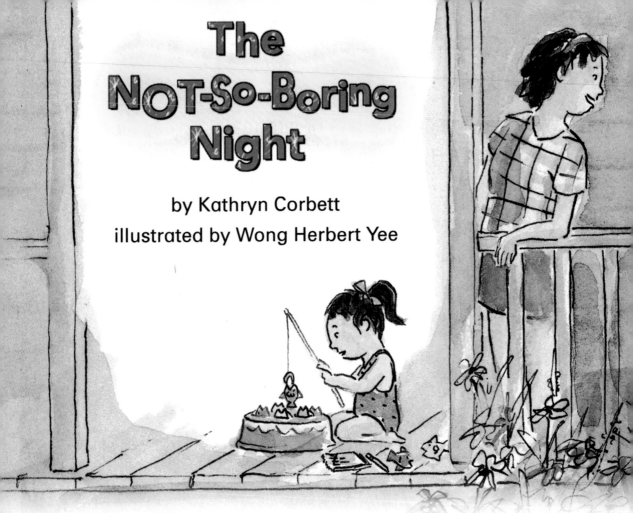

It was a hot night at our summer cabin by the lake. Rose and I were on the porch, playing her fishing game. Mom said, "Jerome, thanks for playing with Rose."

I said, "This game is for little kids. This will be a boring night."

"Maybe not," Mom said. "You like to fish."

"This is not fishing," I said.

I was glad when our Doberman, Duke, barked to go for a walk. I could use a walk myself. "All right, Duke," I said to him. To Mom and Rose I said, "Excuse me. I'll be right back."

"Don't go too close to the lake," Mom called after me.

"No, Mom," I called back, and Duke and I ran off.

"Thanks, Duke!" I said. "That game is so boring. I was starting to doze off, and Rose gets mad when I snore!"

We went down to the cove. I hummed a tune as Duke dug a hole. Then I froze. Someone was by the dunes! I ducked down next to Duke.

It was the farmer we get eggs from for our lunches. Rose and I have fun throwing corn to his chickens.

I supposed it made sense that the farmer would fish here. I'd just never seen him off the farm. But something was very odd. He was throwing back all the fish he got!

Duke and I walked over to the dunes. "I see you're getting lots of fish," I said.

"Oh, yes," the farmer said. "I do very well with this pole." He held it out for me to look at.

I was amazed to see that he was fishing with a magnet!

He swung the pole again and got one
more fish. Something was odd about
the fish, too. It was red, and it had a
number on it! The farmer jotted something
in a little notepad. Then he tossed the fish
back into the lake.

"Excuse me," I asked him, "but why
are you throwing them all back? What
are you putting in your notepad?"

"Oh," he said, "that's my score. I like fishing, but I don't like to take the fish out of the water. So I just make a game of it."

He was adding up his score when I felt a sharp poke.

"Jerome! You're starting to snore," Rose said. I woke up with a plastic fish dangling over my nose. The fish was red, and it had a number on it. Rose giggled.

"Poor Jerome is bored," Mom said. "Come on, you two. Let's walk to the store before it closes and get cones." Rose clapped her hands.

"Okay," I said, "but let's play some more before bed. I like this game better than fishing now."

Sounds All Around

by Susan M. Fischer

illustrated by Donna Ingemanson

Jules was the first to notice that Mrs. Lee was not home. He asked Mr. Jones where she was.

"Mrs. Lee is sick. She went to the hospital," said Mr. Jones. "I hope she will not be there long."

Jules was sad. He liked seeing Mrs. Lee when he walked home from school. She loved to sit and watch the crowd go by.

38

Jules walked down the sidewalk. Mr. Jones was making his chalk art on it. Kids were playing games. Mrs. Peck was selling fruit from her cart. Sue was playing a cool tune on her flute. A dump truck went rushing by.

Then it started to rain. The chalk drawings began to run. Jules listened to the noisy rain. He was thinking hard. Before long, he had a plan.

In the morning there was still a haze from the
rainstorm. Jules went with his mom to see Mrs. Lee.
He had a big bag in his arms.

Mrs. Lee looked a little pale. A nurse fussed
by her bed. When the nurse left, Jules gave
Mrs. Lee a hug. She asked what was in his bag.

40

Jules pulled out some fruit from Mrs. Peck. All the children had made drawings for her. Mr. Jones sent some chalk so Mrs. Lee could make drawings, too.

Mrs. Lee admired her presents. "Thank you, Jules. I miss watching the crowd on the sidewalk. These will keep me from feeling homesick."

Then Jules pulled out the coolest present of all.

He pressed the button on his tape player. The tape played a sound that went *thup, thup, thup.*

"Do you know what that is?" asked Jules. "I'll give you a clue. It's something you can eat."

"It sounds like fruit dropping into a bag," said Mrs. Lee.

"Right! It's this fruit from Mrs. Peck!" said Jules. "Now, what is this?" There was a *whap-thump, whap-thump.*

Mrs. Lee had to think. "It's the kids jumping rope!"

Next there was a loud *bam-bam-zoom.* "That's a truck," she said.

Then the tape played a sweet tune. Mrs. Lee smiled. "That must be Sue!" Jules stood up and mimicked Sue playing the flute.

When the song was over, Mrs. Lee clapped. "Thank you, Jules!" she said. "I was feeling blue. Now I feel as if I'm right there in the crowd."

43

The tape played one more sound. It was a light noise at first, but then it got louder.

"Rain!" Mrs. Lee said. They all listened to the cool sound of rain on the sidewalk.

Mrs. Lee picked up the chalk. She drew a rainbow. Then she put some words under it. *Thank you, my friends. I can't wait to see you all again!*

44

45

by Meish Goldish

illustrated by Laura Ovresat

Hi! I'm Neal. This is Mr. Whiskers, my seal friend. His home is in the sea. You can see my home on the beach.

Mr. Whiskers and I meet here at the beach each weekend. He teaches me about his friends in the ocean. I have a lot of information about seals now.

Mr. Whiskers seems to know all the seals in the ocean. He knows most of the whales, too. He's glad that the sea is so big. If he were in a little pond, he wouldn't have so many friends to greet!

Mr. Whiskers is a good swimmer. He uses his flippers forcibly to reach his top speed. I can swim fast, but not that fast!

Mr. Whiskers and his seal friends swim fast and far. See this map? The seals swam from here to here and didn't get lost. Seals don't need a map!

One time we had a swimming contest to see which seal could swim the fastest. The seals swam out where the sea is deep. I ran along the beach. At first a big seal was in the lead. Then the leader was Mr. Whiskers. He beat all the seals. He was the winner!

Can you see how Mr. Whiskers got his name?
Look at his cheeks. His whiskers help him feel
around in the water. They help him find a good
meal to eat!

Mr. Whiskers has lots of sharp teeth. He uses
them to feast on fish. What a treat for him!

Mr. Whiskers keeps himself very neat. When he comes out of the water, he is so sleek! He would make a very clean pet. But seals can't walk well on land. Their back feet are flippers, too.

Sometimes I wish I were a seal. Swimming all the time would keep me clean. I would never need to take a bath. Now that would be a real treat!

Mom and Dad have never seen Mr. Whiskers. I tell them the details about what we do each weekend.

Dad says, "Sounds like fun, Neal."

Mom says, "How sweet, dear. Now go to sleep."

I know this means they think Mr. Whiskers is not real. They think I see him in my dreams.

This disappoints me a little. I tell them, "Mr. Whiskers is real!"

They just smile. When Mr. Whiskers hears about this, he smiles too. And then, so do I!

story by
Sydnie Meltzer Kleinhenz

illustrated by Joe Cepeda

STAR TIME

Mom and Dad,

Help! Camp could not be worse! I went to my first Stars class. I had my star chart. I wanted to look up at the stars. Do you know what? Stars is for campers who want to <u>be</u> stars. It's not for campers who want to <u>see</u> stars! We all have to perform in a talent show. I prefer watching to acting. I want to quit. Come get me!

Forget it. You'll get this letter after the talent show is over. I'll think of something.

I miss you,
Kirsten

Kirsten could see Karen and Robert recite lines from a play. Carmen and a girl from cabin 2B did handstands. Josh played the camp song on his horn. Jennifer twirled in her costume. Ernest was making up a poem about bugs.

Kirsten sat alone. She looked at her letter. She looked at the river far away. What was she going to do? She went back to her cabin to get her gym bag.

At dusk, Kirsten saw Gilbert. "I do not know what to do for the talent show," he said. "I can't act or make up a poem. I do not know any tricks." He kicked the dirt and hollered, "GROWL!"

"Wow! That was as loud as a dragon," said Kirsten.

"That is my one talent," said Gilbert frowning. "I can be loud."

Kirsten clapped. "I know what we can do!"

Kirsten got her star charts and lantern out of her gym bag. "There are billions of stars," she said. "Some make patterns of things. Look at this."

She stuck a pin into different spots on a card. She put the card over her lantern. It flashed the pattern of stars on a big rock. "Take the lantern. Now do your dragon growl."

Gilbert growled. Kirsten went to the rock and showed Gilbert the pattern in the stars. "Here's the Dragon," she said.

Gilbert and Kirsten got a long, black cloth from the camp director. They pinned it up at the front of the Stars platform. Gilbert helped Kirsten cut spots out of the cloth.

They were all grins when it was their turn at the talent show. Kirsten held her gym bag of props. Gilbert held a funnel to his mouth. They went to the back of the cloth. The campers looked puzzled.

Kirsten flashed her lantern on the back of the cloth. She said, "These are the Big Dipper and the Little Dipper." Gilbert made the sound of dripping water.

For Pegasus, Gilbert made the sound of wings flapping. For the Archer, he made the ping of the string. For the Twins, he made baby sounds. They ended the show with Gilbert's loud growl for the Dragon. The campers clapped and clapped.

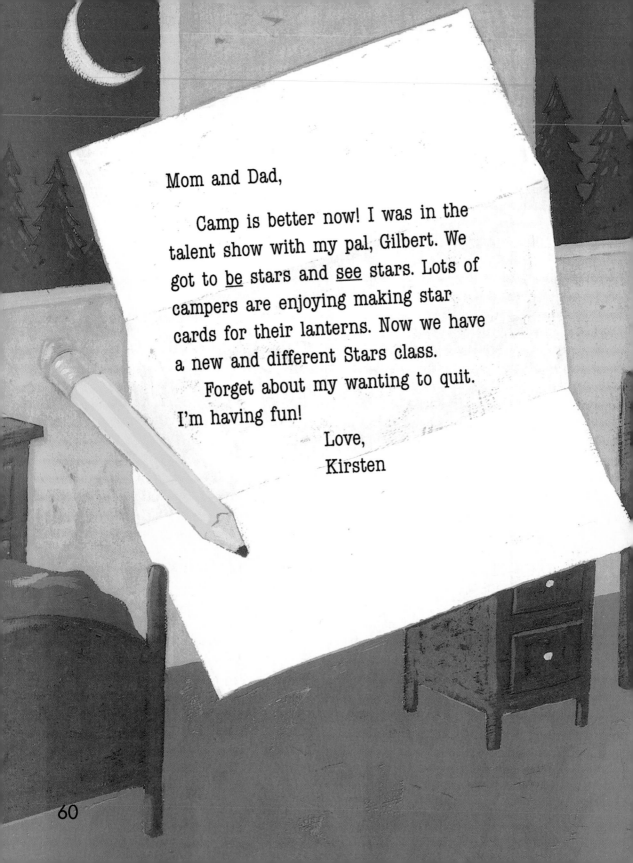

Mom and Dad,

Camp is better now! I was in the talent show with my pal, Gilbert. We got to <u>be</u> stars and <u>see</u> stars. Lots of campers are enjoying making star cards for their lanterns. Now we have a new and different Stars class.

Forget about my wanting to quit. I'm having fun!

Love,
Kirsten

60

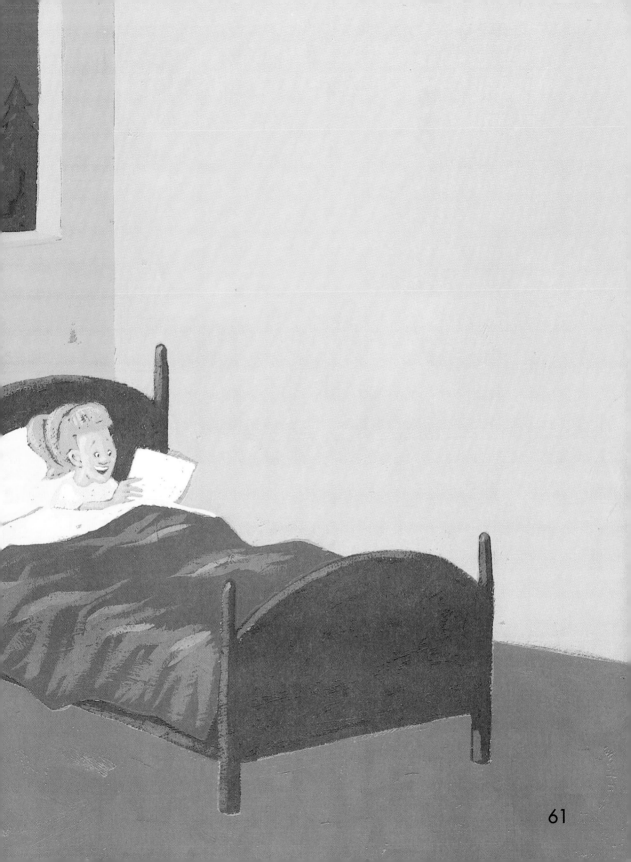

Help on the Trail

by Robert Newell
illustrated by Mike Harper

A chill wind whips the branches. A storm
is coming. Mrs. Arnold's husband, Frank, is out
hunting. Brandon, who is 12, is with him. She
wishes she could telegraph them to come back.

The temperature drops. A bad snowstorm starts. The wind makes the snow hit hard, like splinters.

Are Frank and Brandon lost? They could freeze out there! Did they go north from the ranch or south? Mrs. Arnold can't tell which, but some dogs can.

How do dogs find someone who is lost? They sniff something that belongs to him or her. Then they sniff along the trail, looking for that smell.

Which dogs can do this? Smart dogs. Strong dogs. They have to like adults and children. And they have to have a teacher.

Dogs like this do not just sit and fetch. Starting as pups, they hunt for the teacher over and over.

When someone is lost, dogs like Champ
and Patches start sniffing. They are hunting for
his or her smell. A snowstorm can't stop them
from doing the job. They will find the trail.

This dog stops and barks. It's a signal that he sees someone. ▶

◀ The drifts of snow are up to this dog's chin. She has to inch along. But just watch—she'll get there!

Patches has a red harness and a bell. The bell signals that help is coming. ▶

Help did get to Frank and Brandon Arnold. Some dogs started out at the ranch. They hunted to the north and to the south. They guided friends to the Arnolds. Frank and Brandon had gotten lost. They got chilled, but they did not freeze in the storm.

Frank said, "Thanks so much!" What did Brandon do? He had big, big hugs for the dogs!

THE HUMMINGBIRD ·GARDEN·

Cyrus already knew what Dad would say. He had to ask anyway.

"Dad, may we get a pet? Please! We really need a pet around here."

"You know we can't have a pet," Dad said. "The rule is no dogs in this building. Hamsters make you sneeze, and the city is no place for a pony!"

WRITTEN BY JOSÉ GONZALES
ILLUSTRATED BY JOUNG UN KIM

Cy smiled at Dad's little joke, but he still felt bad.

Then Dad said, "I have an idea. City birds need help. You can use the backyard to make a garden for them. The birds can be your pets."

"Oh, Dad," Cy said. "Our backyard is made of cement! There's no space for a garden out there!" He knew Dad was doing his best, but he didn't understand how that idea could work.

"You can make space," Dad said. "You can use things our neighbors throw out to plant flowers in. You can dig up dirt to put in them. I'll give you a few dollars to get seeds and a bird feeder."

"I'll try it," said Cy. Maybe Dad's idea was not so bad after all.

71

That same evening, Cy looked through bird books.

"I want our bird visitors to be hummingbirds," Cy told Dad.

"Good idea," Dad replied. "Our little garden has ample space for such tiny birds."

"Hummingbirds catch and eat bugs," Cy went on. "They drink the nectar from flowers. Sometimes they drink sweet water from a feeder, too. They like red and pink flowers best, so I'll plant red and pink flowers to attract them to the garden. Once they're here, they'll find the feeder. Then they'll know where to visit when they're thirsty."

Cy looked through the neighbors' junk. He picked up old boxes and pails, then he poked holes in the bottoms so the water would drain out. When Mrs. Cecil found out what he was doing, she gave him old pots from her cellar. Cy filled everything with dirt.

Soon Cy was ready to get his seeds. Dad gave him some money and took him to the shopping center.

Back at home, Cy dug little furrows in the dirt and planted seeds for red flowers. He watered the seeds each day and watched for signs of growth.

73

When Cy spied red flowers in his garden, he mixed up some sweet water. He filled the hummingbird feeder. Then he waited for thirsty hummingbirds.

Cy watched from morning to evening. No little visitors showed up. It seemed that the hummingbirds had shunned his beautiful garden.

Then one summer day Cy spotted a tiny blur. Could it be? Yes! It was a hummingbird. It raced around the garden like a small cyclone. Its wings were going like little windmills. It found the feeder, and soon more hummingbirds joined it.

Each day, Cy's visitors returned. They circled the flowers and sucked sweet water from the feeder. Cy could see their red throats. He looked in his bird book and found that they were ruby-throated hummingbirds.

In the evenings, Cy took down the feeder. He cleaned it out and filled it with fresh sweet water. Then he put it up again. He knew the daytime heat would bring his visitors back.

Cy liked to watch the tiny birds. Their wings went so fast that they were just a blur. They could hang in one place like a helicopter! Cy cherished the time he spent with his new pets.

The days got shorter, and there was less heat. Summer turned to fall. One day the hummingbirds did not return. Cy missed his little pets, but he knew they had to go south. They could not stand winter's snow and ice.

He cleaned the feeder one last time and put it away. He knew he would need it again. Next spring he would plant a new garden. He would put up the feeder, and his pets would visit again. Cy had turned his cement backyard into a very nice place for hummingbirds.

Big Bad Wolf and the Law

by Deborah Eaton   illustrated by Terry Hoff

TIME:

August, some year

PLACE:

Storyland Court

Big Bad Wolf

Judge Bo Peep

Lawyer

Bailiff

Red Riding Cap

78

BAILIFF: Order in the court! All rise for Judge Peep.

JUDGE PEEP: Be seated. Let's launch right into this. What is the charge?

LAWYER (*hands judge a paper*): Attempted eating, Judge.

JUDGE (*discards paper*): Well, that's original. Usually eating is acceptable, isn't it?

LAWYER: Yes, but Mr. Wolf was found chasing a grandma and her little granddaughter.

JUDGE: That's awful!

WOLF (*worried*): I didn't do it!

JUDGE: Well, let's get on with it. I've been up since dawn (*yawns*), and I've got lost sheep that have to be caught.

BAILIFF: Mr. Big B. Wolf! Please stand and raise your right paw.

WOLF *(paw up)*: I'm honored to be here, Your Honor. Allow me to say that I never saw such a beautiful judge.

LAWYER: I object! Attempted flattery!

JUDGE: I'll allow it. *(looks in pocket mirror)* It shows he's truthful. Now, call your first witness.

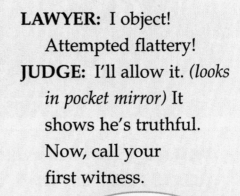

BAILIFF: Little Red Riding Cap!

LAWYER: What caused you to accuse the wolf, Miss Cap?

RED CAP: He . . . he . . . *(begins to bawl)*

LAWYER: He what?

RED CAP: He said my grandma would be *delicious*! *(cries louder)*

LAWYER *(triumphantly)*: You see? He did it!

WOLF *(desperately)*: No! I didn't! I'm innocent!

JUDGE *(chin in hand)*: I'm so worried about my sheep.

WOLF: Sheep? Sheep are delicious, too. Usually I like them in mint sauce, but . . .

JUDGE: That's it. HE DID IT!

LAWYER: And he isn't even repentant!

BAILIFF: Haul him off to jail!

WOLF: Wait! This is such an injustice! It's the author's fault, not mine! I was just following the original script! My name is really Big *Bill* Wolf! I'm a real sweet pea!

LAWYER: Ha! Ha! Tell us another one!

WOLF: It's the truth! I'm a victim of circumstances. We all are! Just look at you, Judge! You *can't* like that ruffled dress and awkward bonnet. You have them on because they're drawn on you in every story.

JUDGE: Well, I . . .

WOLF: And you! *(points a claw at Red Riding Cap)* Do you really want to go to your grandma's all the time? Wouldn't you rather go bowling or something?

RED CAP: Bowling?

WOLF: Aw, I'd never eat the kid, Judge. I'd never put a paw on her.

JUDGE: So you didn't eat my sheep?

WOLF: Why, I wouldn't hurt a flea. *(scratches)* I'm not big and bad, just ask my mother. Ask anyone!

LAWYER: Let's ask my surprise witnesses. *(nods to bailiff)*

JUDGE: Who are they?

BAILIFF: The three little pigs!

WOLF *(sinking into chair)*: Uh-oh.

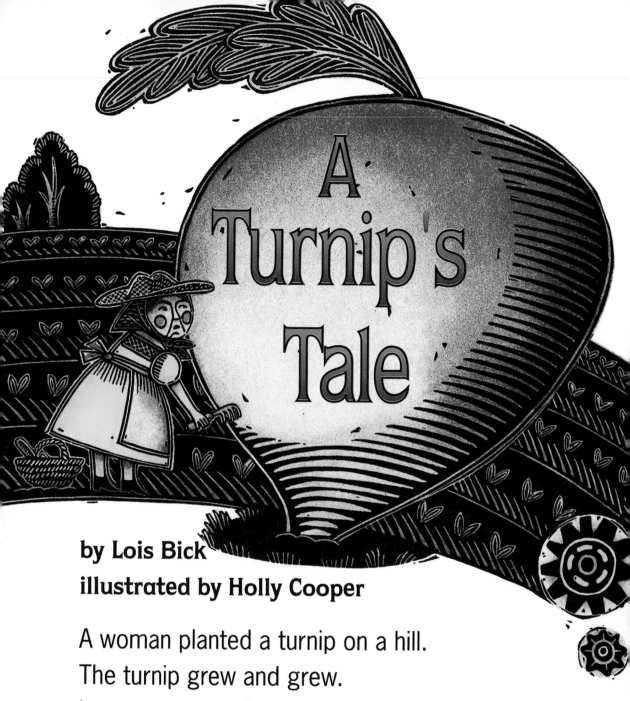

A Turnip's Tale

by Lois Bick

illustrated by Holly Cooper

A woman planted a turnip on a hill.
The turnip grew and grew.
It was enormous!
It got so big it tipped over.
Then down, down, down the hill it fell.

86

The turnip fell into a well.
What a mess!
"Oh, no! That turnip is in my well!"
the woman yelled. "I have to get it out!"

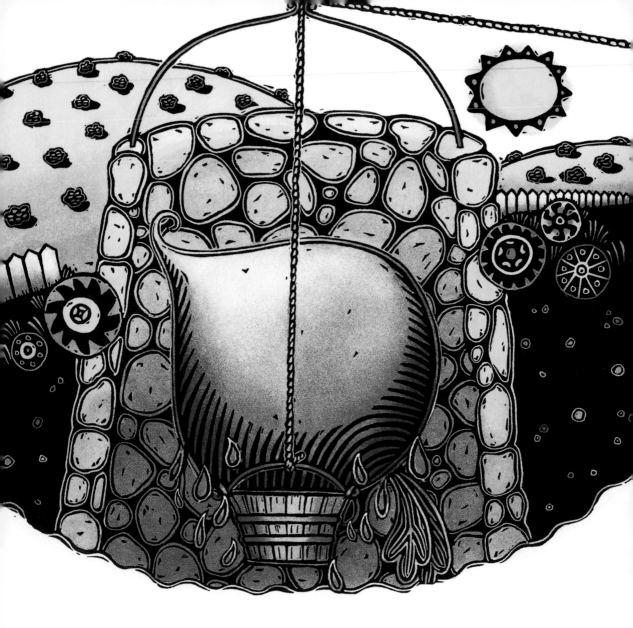

The woman pulled and pulled. Then she pulled again.

But she could not get the turnip out of the well.

She called for help.

"I will help," her granddaughter said.

The woman and her granddaughter pulled
and pulled. Then they pulled again.

But they could not get the turnip
out of the well.

The granddaughter called for help.

"We will help," some men said.

The woman and her granddaughter and the
men pulled and pulled. Then they pulled again.

But they could not get the turnip
out of the well.

The men called for help.

"I can help," said a mouse.
"You?" the woman asked.
"You are a little pest. You are
not strong."

"Well, I will do my best,"
the mouse said. "Look. Then do
what I do."

The mouse bent over the well.
Then all the rest helped.

Yes! They got the turnip out!
The woman was so glad!
The granddaughter clapped her hands.
The men sat down to rest.
The little mouse had a big grin.
He did his best, and he got that turnip out!

When You Visit Relatives

by Hector Morales
illustrated by Sandra Shap

Call First

If you want to visit your relatives, don't forget to call them first. Let them know your travel plans. They will have to get ready for company. Pick out a nice present to take to them.

Ask a Companion to Join You

Instead of traveling alone, you might invite a friend to come along. First you should ask your relatives if it's okay. Don't make it a surprise!

Get Out Those Wheels

How will you get there? Biking is fine if it's not far and the weather is good. Avoid traffic. Travel on safe roads.

Don't forget to take along some snacks. You will probably get hungry.

Get Out That Luggage

Pack sturdy clothes and toys—enough for several days. Travel light so you don't put too much on your bicycle.

Don't let bad weather spoil your trip. Remember to take your raincoat. Dry travelers are happy travelers.

Follow the Rules

Handle your own luggage.

Wipe your feet on the mat.

Keep your cassette player turned low.

Don't jump on the bed.

Don't eat in bed.

Don't make a lot of noise.

DON'T STAY TOO LONG!

Help Out

Don't just sit around. Offer to help with the chores.

Make your bed each day. Pick up your toys. Make lunches for everyone. Wash the dishes, too. Your relatives will be happy to have your help.

Say Thank You

Tell your relatives what a good time you had. Thank them for having you. Then invite them to visit you soon.

Make a point of writing a thank-you note when you get home. Your relatives will remember your visit with joy!

A NEW BEST FRIEND

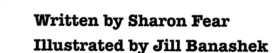

Written by Sharon Fear
Illustrated by Jill Banashek

"Write to me!" Howard shouted.

"I will!" Rick shouted back. The car and the moving van started off. They went down the block, around the playground, and beyond it.

Rick was moving to a new town.

"I wish I could go, too," Howard said to his friend Beth.

"Will you be lonely without him?" asked Beth.

"He was my BEST friend," Howard said

100 seriously.

"Help me with my kite," said Beth. Howard held the kite. Beth unwound some string. She fastened the string to the kite.

"You can get a new best friend," said Beth. Howard frowned. "How? Who?"

Howard's dog bounded up to them. Beth picked up a stick and tossed it. "Get it, Bow Wow!" Beth shouted.

"How about Jack?" she asked.

"Jack does not like Bow Wow," Howard said.

"How about Norman?" said Beth.

"Norman who?" asked Howard.

"His dad has a brown mustache," said Beth.

"Bow Wow does not like Norman," said Howard.

Bow Wow growled.

102 "See," said Howard.

Howard picked up his basketball, dribbled it, and shot. It rimmed around and fell out. He passed it to Beth. She dribbled around him. She shot. Pow! She sank it!

"Wow!" shouted Howard. "Outstanding!"

"I have a secret gift," teased Beth. They played on trading shots.

"Chuck!" she said. "Chuck could be your new best friend."

Howard frowned. "Chuck can't play basketball," he said. "Not like you."

"How about Ben?" said Beth.
"Can't swim," said Howard.
"Patrick?" said Beth.
"Can't play chess," said Howard.
"Carl!" shouted Beth.
"Can't do a cartwheel," said Howard.
"I give up," said Beth, doing a cartwheel.
104

Then it came to him. Beth was his friend. She was a girl, but she was the best.

"How about you?" Howard said.

She looked at him. "Can you dribble with your left hand?" she teased again.

"Yes," said Howard.

"You wish!" She laughed out loud. "Well, let's work on it now." She passed him the basketball.

"Outstanding!" said Howard.

Zelda
Moves to the Desert

by Linda Lott
illustrated by Tim Bowers

Each night, Zelda the bat went flying. She worked hard to find food. She ate bug after bug.

One morning, as Zelda returned home, a gentle rain was falling. Zelda was tired and wet when she reached her cozy cave. She folded her wings. The little creek sang to her as she drifted off to sleep.

As Zelda slept, the rain fell harder and the creek got bigger. The water rose higher, right up to the ledge of her cozy cave.

When night came, Zelda woke up. The water had begun to come in. Her home would soon be flooded. Zelda peeked over the edge of the ledge. She dropped a rock into the water and it sank far down. The water was deep!

107

The creek was rushing past the cave very quickly. Zelda watched a bottle drift past. Then some little mice floated by in a bowl. They were using it as a boat. "You'd better find a new home, Zelda!" the mice shouted.

Zelda sighed. She realized that the mice were right. "My cave is not cozy anymore," she said to herself. "It is not even safe. I must find a new home that is safe and dry."

Giant clouds were still looming when
Zelda launched herself from the ledge. First
she flapped her way into the forest.

"It's too damp in here!" said Zelda.
"This is not a good home for me."

Next Zelda fluttered out over the sea. She looked down at a fleet of boats bobbing on the waves. They had sails of bright colors.

"The sailboats on the dark sea look like little gems on black velvet," said Zelda. "But the sea is not a good home for me. It's much too wet!"

110

Zelda kept on flying as the sun started to rise over the horizon. Suddenly she spotted sand below. She realized she was over the desert.

"The desert is very dry," Zelda said. "I think I have found just the right spot for me!"

As morning came, Zelda slid under a ledge in a tiny cave. She slept well in her dry, cozy new home.

The Case of the Strange Sculptor

by Lisa Eisenberg • illustrated by Kenneth Spengler

It was an important day in the village of Fudge Corners. All the citizens had come to the village square to see the work of a local sculptor revealed. Gina Ginetti, well-known girl detective, was there with her friends Angela and Al.

"I'm so excited!" Angela exclaimed. "Today's the day we get to see Reggie Rodgers's statue of the Gentle Giant. It's supposed to be his finest work yet!"

"I don't see what all the fuss is about," Al muttered.

"The Gentle Giant is Fudge Corners's best-known dog!" Angela retorted. "He saved the life of the village's founder, Felix Fudge, in 1809."

"The Gentle Giant is fine," said Al. "It's Reggie Rodgers I don't like. He got first prize in the art show last year, and he's bragged about it ever since!"

Angela frowned. "Maybe the reason you don't like Reggie is that he's a better sculptor than you are!"

"*I'm* the better sculptor," Al insisted. "*He's* just the better boaster."

"Oh, stop arguing, you two," Gina broke in. "Look! They're about to unveil the statue!"

The mayor of Fudge Corners retold the story of how the Gentle Giant had saved Felix Fudge. He also spoke about how lucky their village was to have a fine sculptor like Reggie Rodgers. Then he swept away the sheet that had hidden the statue.

"Ohhhh," cried the crowd. "The dog looks so lifelike! What a genius Rodgers is!" A flock of pigeons fluttered down to investigate.

Everyone clapped, except for Al. His mouth dropped open and he gaped at the platform. "That's *my* statue of the Gentle Giant! I made it in my basement, and it was still there last night. Someone stole it, and I know who's guilty. Reggie Rodgers, that's who!"

Angela put her arm around her excited friend. "Come on now, Al. We know you don't like Reggie Rodgers, but that's no reason to make up wild stories!"

"I *did* make it! I wanted to see if I could do a better job than Reggie. I was certain I could," declared Al.

Angela glanced nervously around the crowded square. "Everyone is looking at us strangely. You'd better pipe down, Al."

"Wait a second, Angela," Gina put in. "I can't remember Al ever telling a lie. I believe him!"

"What reason could Reggie have for taking Al's statue?" Angela asked. "It doesn't seem logical."

"I don't know, but I trust my detective's instinct," Gina said. "Let's find him and talk to him straightaway!"

Al found the support of Gina and Angela strengthening as they searched the large crowd. When they located Reggie Rodgers, Al marched right up to him. "Why did you steal my statue?" he asked.

Reggie sneered. "Ha! Why would I sneak into your basement and steal your sad little statue?"

"I don't know!" Al yelled. "Maybe yours didn't come out right, or maybe you didn't finish on time."

Reggie glanced around nervously. "That's crazy! I don't even know where you live, and besides, I have an alibi for last night."

"I've done it again!" Gina bragged. "I've cracked another case. Reggie, whatever your alibi is for last night, it's a fake. *You* know you stole Al's statue, and *I* know you're guilty. You gave yourself away twice!"

How did Gina know that Reggie had stolen Al's statue?

Solution: Reggie said he didn't know where Al lived, but he knew the statue had been in the basement. Also, he knew the statue had been stolen last night!

BUG CATCHERS

by Robert Newell
illustrated by Doug Bowles

BROWN BAT

Brown Bat is my name, and bug-catching is my game! Come along and watch me in action. Marshes are my favorite places to hunt. The boggiest marshes, where water oozes up through the mud, are the best because they have the most mosquitoes. I'm headed in the direction of a boggy marsh right now. It's a dark, moonless night, but that won't slow me down.

I screech as I fly. When I hear the sound bounce back, I know the location of my next victim.

It's a big mosquito! Swoop! I catch it in my wing. Now watch this flipping motion. I toss the bug up, up, right into my mouth.

Crunch!

On an ordinary night, I eat about half my own weight in bugs. Does that convince you that I'm a super bug catcher?

BOLAS SPIDER

Spiders are bug catchers, too. Ordinary spiders use webs, but not me. I use a different invention.

First I perch on a branch by the garden shed, where fertilizers and bug chemicals are stored. Then I let a silky string ooze from my spinnerets. I add a sticky blob to one end to make a bolas, like the ones South American cowboys use. Then I get into position.

What I do next takes great skill and concentration. I don't see well, but I can feel when moths fly by. They have no notion that I'm here. When one comes close, I quickly toss my bolas in its direction.

I got one!

The moth is tangled in the bolas string. When I pull it in, it's dinner time!

Sometimes I wrap my catch in silk and hang it up to eat later. These roll-ups make great convenience foods for days when I accidentally miss with my bolas. I simply inject a little of my bug-dissolving solution into a prepackaged meal. Then I sip up a delicious dinner.

PRAYING MANTIS

Why fly back and forth all night or struggle with a tangled, sticky string? I catch bugs by holding still and letting them come to me.

First I have to make a decision about where to wait. Today I station myself on a twig near the ground.

I sit motionless, still as a stone. I have five eyes, and my good vision helps me watch for victims.

Here comes a beetle!

I wait, and I wait some more. When the beetle is very close, I pounce. Each of my front legs snaps shut at the joint like a steel trap. The beetle's reaction is to kick and wiggle, but it's useless for it to struggle. I will never let go of my dinner.

I will eat the beetle, but I will still be hungry. I am always hungry. Luckily, there are always more bugs.

OTHER BUG CATCHERS

I catch bugs, too, but I have no intention of eating any. No chocolate-covered ants for me, thank you! I just look at the bugs and let them go.

Anteaters slurp up ants. Fish and frogs gulp down flies. Foxes avoid starvation by eating grubs when they must. All these carnivorous creatures help keep the insect population down, and I'm convinced that's a good thing. After all, how many mosquitoes and flies do you want in your backyard?

Thank you, bug catchers!

Mr. Carver's Carrots

by Cassidy James   illustrated by Ellen Sasaki

The summer day was hot. The flowers were wilted. Mr. Carver and Ben were damp and wrinkled all over.

"I'm hungry for carrots," said Mr. Carver.

"Sounds good," said Ben. "I wish we had planted some carrot seeds."

"What are we waiting for?" asked Mr. Carver.

Mr. Carver got some carrot seeds. Then he began to dig up the ground.

Ben knelt down. He dropped the little seeds into the soil. He put more soil on top. Now the seeds were snug beneath the dark soil.

One day a storm came. It started as a shower. Then big drops plopped down. They fell faster and faster. They sounded louder and louder.

After the storm, Ben ran outdoors. Had the seeds floated away? No! Little sprouts had popped up. Ben was proud.

130

A heat spell came next. The summer sun
pounded down. The carrot sprouts shimmered in
the heat.

Ben and Mr. Carver began a relay race to help
the sprouts. Ben filled buckets. Mr. Carver lugged
them around the garden.

At last! The day they had waited for came. Ben
pulled on the tops of the carrots. One by one, big,
beautiful carrots popped out of the ground. Ben made
a tower of carrots.

Ben and Mr. Carver crunched and munched. They
made a lot of noise.

Then Ben said, "Carrots are good, but you can have too many carrots!"

"You're right," said Mr. Carver. "Now I'm hungry for watermelon."

"Sounds good," said Ben. "What are we waiting for?"

The Music Maker

by Sydnie Meltzer Kleinhenz
illustrated by Roberta Ludlow

Wherever Dwight went, his drumsticks went, too. He tapped on anything he could find. He liked to try new ways to make his rhythms sound better.

Dwight spotted some rubber bands on the playground. He wound them around the ends of two sticks. He twisted them into tight rubber balls. Then he used them to beat a rhythm on his boxes.

"What are you doing?" Jon asked.

"I'm trying to get the right sound," Dwight answered. He tapped on the plastic bucket.

"You need good drumsticks to make a good sound," Jon said. "Those look mighty bad to me."

"They just aren't right for this bucket drum," Dwight said. "Maybe I'll try them on something else."

Dwight spotted a garbage can on the playground. He drummed on the garbage can's lid. BANG-BANG-BANG! The loud sound startled the children nearby. They put their hands over their ears. Jon's friend Linda appeared at his side.

"What are you doing, Dwight?" she asked. "You gave me such a fright!"

"I'm working on the notes of my music,"
Dwight answered. "I'm going to play 'The Star-Spangled Banner' at the baseball game Saturday night."

Linda sighed. "You must mean you'll drum out the beat," she said. "You can't play the notes of 'The Star-Spangled Banner' on a drum."

Jon giggled. "You need a trumpet or a flute to play real music," he said. He imitated a trumpet player.

"MY drum CAN make real music," Dwight answered. "Come over to my house after school, and I'll show you."

Dwight's dad had a workshop behind the house. Jon and Linda watched him heat a big steel can. He hammered shapes into the top of it and then put it in water. This created clouds of steam. When he pulled it out of the water, he tapped on the shapes. To Jon and Linda's surprise, notes sounded. "That drum does make music!" said Jon.

On Saturday night, Jon and Linda went to the baseball game. Before the game began, the conductor lifted his arms high. All the fans got up. Then the band started playing "The Star-Spangled Banner." Dwight delighted the crowd as he made music on his steel drum.

THE LITTLE LIGHTHOUSE

By Kaye Gager

Illustrated by Jui Ishida

Today is a sad day for my family and me. We are going to a new home. We listen for a storm, but the water is still. Then we get into the boat and quietly float away. The little lighthouse is left all alone.

I watch the light glow in the mist. I am sorry to leave the little lighthouse that was my home.

I will miss helping look for boats lost in the fog. Our family kept the light on, night and day, for boats to see.

"The lighthouse will miss us," I say.

My family all agree.

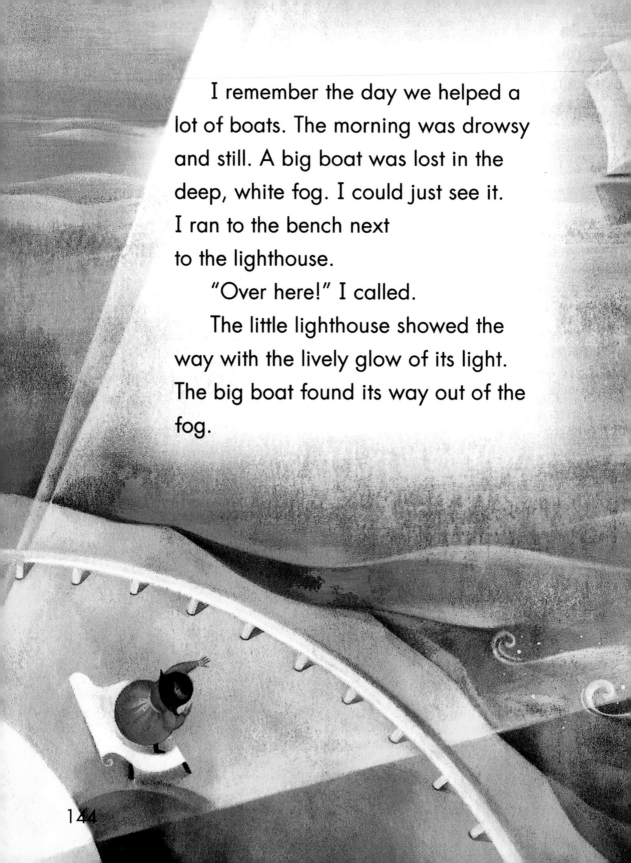

I remember the day we helped a lot of boats. The morning was drowsy and still. A big boat was lost in the deep, white fog. I could just see it. I ran to the bench next to the lighthouse.

"Over here!" I called.

The little lighthouse showed the way with the lively glow of its light. The big boat found its way out of the fog.

Then a little boat sailed too close
to the shore. It was about to hit the
rocks because it couldn't see in the
fog.

"Stay away!" I shouted. "You're
too close to the rocks!" With a gentle
roar of its horn, the lighthouse agreed.

The little boat turned around and
sailed away safely.

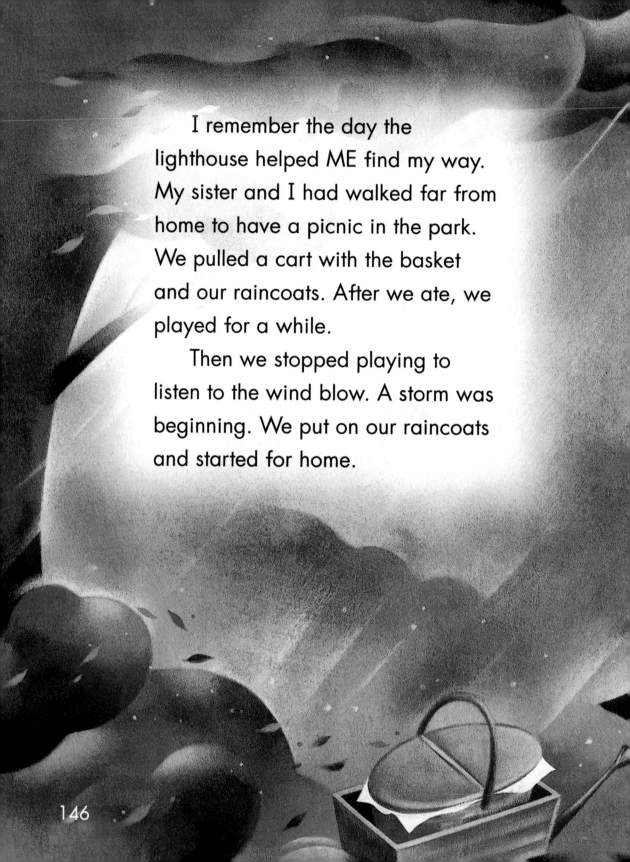

I remember the day the lighthouse helped ME find my way. My sister and I had walked far from home to have a picnic in the park. We pulled a cart with the basket and our raincoats. After we ate, we played for a while.

Then we stopped playing to listen to the wind blow. A storm was beginning. We put on our raincoats and started for home.

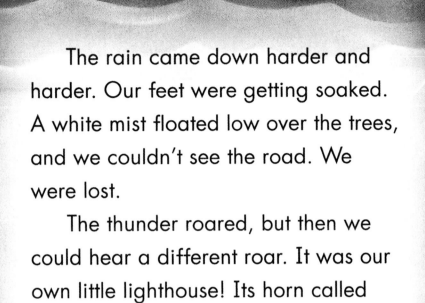

The rain came down harder and harder. Our feet were getting soaked. A white mist floated low over the trees, and we couldn't see the road. We were lost.

The thunder roared, but then we could hear a different roar. It was our own little lighthouse! Its horn called out to us again and again. We listened and followed the sound until we found our way home.

Now a new family will come to the lighthouse. They will watch for lost boats. They will keep the light on, night and day. Maybe there will be a new girl to pay attention to lost boats. Maybe she will stand on the bench and call to them the way I did.

I hope the new family will love
the little lighthouse, too. I know that
my sister and I will listen to it in
our dreams.

While the Bear SLEEPS

by Deborah Akers
illustrated by Douglas Bowles

The bear is snug in his den, but the mouse must work. This morning, she is out looking for seeds. Last autumn she hid some in the dirt. Today she must find them. She digs and digs in the ground. Where are the seeds?

It is the dusky end of the day. The glowing sun has pointed out the seeds, and the mouse has found them. Now her family is fed. Her children curl up in her fur. Tomorrow the mouse must go again to get seeds. Outdoors, a storm is beginning.

The bear is snug in his den, but the bird must work. The wind is strong this morning. It is natural for the bird to fly very far. At last she sees something red on some thorns in the snow. Perfect!

It is the dusky end of the day. The bird rests as the storm swirls around her. She is fed for today and will not stir until tomorrow. Then she will fly back to the thorns for more.

The bear is snug in his den, but the rabbit must work. Today he is very hungry. He cannot find any leaves. The trees are completely empty. He digs in the snow to turn up some old, brown grass. What is this in the dirt? Here is a new little sprout. There are three more!

It is the dusky end of the day. The rabbit hops home.
Today was a perfect day. He found many new plants, and
tomorrow there will be more. He knows his waiting for the
snow to melt is over.

After the snow melts, a sliver of sun will find the
bear's den. The bear will stir from his long nap and smell
the wet soil. When he knows a new day is beginning . . .

. . . the bear will get up. But look out!

He will be VERY, VERY hungry!

SPACE TRIP

by Caren B. Stelson
illustrated by
Wayne Vincent

Hello, everyone! I'm Paula Planet of Universe
Space Trips. I'll be your space guide. Is everyone
ready? Fasten your space belts—it's the law!

It's time to launch our Space Trip Ship.

10, 9, 8, 7, 6, 5, 4, 3, 2, 1 . . .

Blast off!

Today you are in for a treat. We will see Earth, the blue planet.

Look out your window. You can see planet Earth coming closer. Do you see why Earth is called the blue planet? All that blue on it is water. In fact, most of Earth's surface is liquid. The brown and green places are land. You can see white clouds and white patches of ice, too. Sometimes you can even see lightning. Isn't Earth beautiful?

Assemble your Space Scopes, everyone. Look closely at Earth. Do you see all the different kinds of people, animals, and plants? You won't find those on any of the other planets. Only Earth has the air, soil, and water they need. Now turn your Space Scopes to the sun. Be careful—it's awfully bright! The sun's heat is intense. It would be too dangerous for us to visit there. Earth is the third planet from the sun. The planets closer to the sun are too hot for us to live on. Those farther away are too cold. Being the third planet from the sun makes Earth just right for the people, plants, and animals that live on it.

162

Now look at Earth again. Do you see that it is spinning, or rotating? It rotates once every 24 hours. That's what causes night and day. Notice how the sun's light reflects off Earth's surface. It is dawn there. Now notice where it is dark. It is night in those places. As Earth rotates, it is day and then night. Soon the dark side will turn to the light and have dawn. The light side will turn away from the light and become dark. It will be night there.

It takes one year for Earth to orbit the Sun. That sounds as slow as a crawl, but it's really very fast. Earth moves at 67,000 miles an hour. It travels almost 100 miles on its path while you count to five!

Let's land on Earth's moon and take a short rest. The moon is only about 240,000 miles away from Earth. We will be there in no time. There is no air or liquid on the moon. You must haul your own in your space pack when you get off. There is a gift shop near the launch pad that sells postcards. You can write home about what you saw today—the beautiful planet Earth!

AN AMAZING FEAT

by Susan M. Fischer

illustrated by Bryn Barnard

Amelia Earhart is an American heroine. She became a pilot when flying was still new. In those days, there were not many women pilots. Amelia Earhart decided that she would be one. Once Amelia decided something, she would not give up. She refused to sit at home. She wanted to show that women could do more.

166

Amelia was eleven when she first came upon an airplane at a fair. That was the place where she fell in love with flying.

When Amelia was a teenager, a war started, and she helped as a nurse. She watched the pilots and listened to the plane engines roar. After the war she decided she wanted to fly herself.

Amelia had some money from her
grandmother. This let her take the flying lessons
she wanted. She was even able to get her own
plane, the *Friendship*. In it she flew higher than any
woman had flown.

Soon flying was the center of Amelia's life. She flew to places all over the world. She was the first woman to fly across the Atlantic alone. What an amazing feat! Later she set new records for speed and distance.

Amelia Earhart became well-known around the world. Spectators came to cheer when she took off and landed. Amelia thanked the people of each city for their hospitality.

Amelia had one more dream. It would be an even more amazing feat. She wanted to fly all the way around the world!

In 1937, when she was forty years old, she got her chance. This time she would take her friend Fred Noonan. A partner would add weight but would be needed on such a long trip.

Together they filled the tanks with gasoline and checked the engines. As they took off, spectators stood and watched with pride and hope.

The plane had flown most of the way when it ran out of fuel. Amelia Earhart, her partner, and her plane disappeared. Hundreds of people have looked for them ever since. The plane has never been found.

Amelia Earhart said of her flying, "The dreams of long ago had come true." She showed everyone that to live your dream, you must never give up. Amelia Earhart is a heroine to celebrate.